COVENANT • BIBLE • STUDIES

Exodus
Freed for the
Journey with God

Connie Burkholder

faithQuest® ♦ Brethren Press®

Contents

Foreword

The Covenant Bible Studies series provides *relational Bible studies* for people who want to study the Bible in small groups rather than alone.

Relational Bible study differs from other types of study. Relational Bible study is anchored in the story of God's covenant with the people of the Old Testament, the new covenant in Jesus Christ, and the covenant community that is the church today. This style of Bible study is for small groups of people who can meet face-to-face on a regular basis and covenant to support one another and grow together in an intimate group.

Relational Bible study takes seriously a corporate faith, a faith that relies on the contributions of all members. As each person contributes to study, prayer, and work, the group becomes the real body of Christ alive in the world. Each one's contribution is needed and important. "For just as the body is one and has many members, and all the members of the body, though many, are one body, so it is with Christ. . . . Now you are the body of Christ and individually members of it" (1 Cor. 12:12, 17).

Relational Bible study helps both individuals and the group to claim the promise of the Spirit and the working of the Spirit. As one person testified, "In our commitment to one another and in our sharing, something happened. . . . We were woven together in love by the Master Weaver. It is something that can happen only when two or three or seven are gathered in God's name and we understand the promise of God's presence in our lives."

In the small group environment, members aid one another in seeking to become

- Biblically informed so as to better understand the revelation of God;
- Globally aware of the interconnectedness of God's world;
- Relationally sensitive to God, self, and others.

Groups that use this study can build up the body of Christ and deepen faith by

- gathering as a small group of learners, open to God's word and committed to discerning its meaning;
- allowing the words, stories, and admonitions found in scripture to come alive for today, challenging and renewing us;
- thinking of all people as learners and all as leaders and appreciating the contributions of all;
- deeply respecting the courage and vulnerability of each person as he or she shares out of experience.

Each Sharing and Prayer section is intended for use in the hour preceding the Bible study to foster intimacy in the covenant group and relate personal sharing to the Bible study topic, preparing one another to go out again in all directions as people of faith in the world.

Welcome to this study. As you search the scriptures, may you also search yourself. May God's voice and guidance and the love and encouragement of brothers and sisters in Christ challenge you to live more fully the abundant life God promises.

Preface

In memory of my mother, Mary Helen,
and in honor of my father, Raymond,
whose lives in the church and faith in God
provided the foundation for my faith journey.

You are about to embark on a journey through Exodus! Although many of the Exodus passages will be familiar, perhaps you will encounter some passages that are new to you. I pray that you will approach each session with openness of mind and spirit. Together, we will rediscover the depth of God's love in calling the Hebrew slaves to become the people called Israel.

Most of our lessons include a significant amount of scripture text. In these lessons we cannot possibly digest every theological nugget that flows through these rich passages. I invite you to expand your own learning beyond what can be discussed during your group time. For my preparation in writing these lessons, I primarily used two commentary sources: Waldemar Janzen's *Exodus* in the Believers Church Bible Commentary series and Walter Brueggemann's commentary on Exodus in *The New Interpreter's Bible, Volume I*. Both writers share scholarly information along with helpful reflections on living faithfully. I recommend these resources to you.

The Book of Exodus is not intended as a detailed account of everything that happened during this segment of the Hebrew people's history. Instead, it chronicles specific highlights of Israel's tumultuous relationship with God as the people flee Egypt and travel to the Promised Land. These stories invite us to reflect on God's nature and consider the ways in which the travelers responded to their circumstances. We are then invited to reflect on our own lives and faith, considering how we might grow closer to the Holy One who willingly guides us.

When God is in the picture, change is sure to happen—change that brings justice and truth, wholeness and liberation. In this study, we will discover God's intention to be in relationship with people. God truly desires to know the people and to be known by them as well. Entering into the witness of these stories opens us to be known and shaped by this same God.

Discover God, who so frequently surprises us when we step out in faith. In many ways the Exodus story parallels our own spiritual journeys. Do we invite God to lead us into unknown territory, or do we complain when climbing over rocky terrain? Get ready to journey. Be open. Be present. Be transformed!

Blessings for the journey,

Connie R. Burkholder

1

A Desperate Situation and Five Gutsy Females
Exodus 1:1–2:10

Personal Preparation

1. Pray for God's Spirit to lead as you begin this study. Pray that your group might become closer to God and one another as you journey together.
2. Read the introduction in this study guide and explore the recommended Bible commentaries to help you understand the story of Exodus as a whole—while getting a sense of the overarching themes in this foundational story. Then read the scripture and the lesson material for this week.
3. Reflect on your own faith journey, remembering difficulties or transitions. Prayerfully remember people who helped something new come to life in you. Give thanks to God.

Suggestions for Sharing and Prayer

1. Begin this journey through Exodus by introducing yourselves in a new way. Tell the group about the meaning or history of your name. How has your name influenced your understanding of who you are?
2. Share about a defining or transforming moment in your life—an event after which you might declare, "I was never the same again."

3. Pray for God's guidance as you begin this Exodus journey together.
4. Talk together briefly about what's going on in your life. What joys, needs, transitions, struggles, or accomplishments are present now? Listen respectfully to each person, holding their stories in reverence and confidence. Allow for some moments of quiet reflection between each person's sharing.
5. Pray together as a group, giving each joy or concern to God.

Understanding

When I reflect upon my years in congregational ministry, I can recall a number of stories that reveal something about each congregation's personality and commitment to ministry and mission. Every congregation has defining moments that become part of the group's collective memory and provide insightful glimpses into community values and beliefs.

The Book of Exodus describes several pivotal events in the Judeo-Christian tradition that define the Israelites as a people. God led the Hebrew people out of Egypt, and they organized as a worshiping community in relationship to the God who had created them. This was the same Creator who had given promises, blessings, and responsibilities to Abraham and Sarah. Our first lesson from Exodus 1:1–2:10 provides the scenario for the story, telling us how the Egyptian ruler has ruthlessly enslaved the Hebrew people, but fertile seeds of hope are planted in the events surrounding Moses' birth.

The Names Have Disappeared

The opening verses connect Exodus with the story of Genesis. Joseph, his eleven brothers, and his father are named. The narrator relates that over time, their contemporaries died and their descendants multiplied prolifically in Egypt. Then the narrator introduces a new king. This pharaoh is believed to be Sethos I, father of Ramses II. The term *pharaoh* is an Egyptian title that is used interchangeably with the word *king*. This king/pharaoh does not know Joseph. This is not surprising, as biblical scholars report that he lived about four hundred years after Joseph did. Scholars estimate the time period of the Exodus as 1350-1200 BCE. Thus, something more is implied here.

The story of Joseph and his role in saving Egypt from famine has been forgotten (see Gen. 41). The people have failed to keep Joseph's story alive. Joseph's name, in a sense, has disappeared. In fact, note the significant absence of names in the Hebrew narrative in verses 1:5-14. The "Hebrews" are grouped together without any individual identifiers as we discover Pharaoh's fear of them. Names hold power and give people a unique identity—a personal identity that the people have lost. Even God's name is hardly mentioned in this part of the story.

The Hebrew people's very existence becomes jeopardized because the names have disappeared, their story has not been told, and the witness about God has gone silent. This new king has no reason to value the Hebrew people. He does not know who they are. But the growing population of Hebrew people poses a threat to the pharaoh. With some level of paranoia, he ruthlessly enslaves them as forced laborers. When the Hebrew people continue to multiply, Pharaoh does the unthinkable. He imposes an order of genocide for all male Hebrew babies. Perhaps genocide is more likely when the aggressor does not know the names of the victims.

Enter the Midwives
The first few verses of this book describe a desperate situation. It is when the midwives enter the story that the names reappear. We hear their names—Shiphrah and Puah—and we learn that Shiphrah and Puah know something of God. These women "fear" God or, more accurately translated, are in awe of God. They defy the king's orders and refuse to kill the Hebrew people's male infants. With this act of civil disobedience, these women choose life.

In his commentary on Exodus, Waldemar Janzen underscores the significance of the midwives in this story. He notes that "the shrewdness of Pharaoh is deliberately matched and neutralized here by the shrewd reply of the midwives. God blesses the midwives and gives them families, making them a sign: Those who align themselves with God's plans will themselves become a part of these plans. . . . Let us note that God's plan of salvation is initiated here by women. In contrast to the unnamed Pharaoh, they are both named—a sign of dignity and importance" (39).

The action of Shiphrah and Puah allows the story to unfold further with the story of Moses' birth. Pharaoh sees his plan hasn't worked, so now he tells *all* his people to eliminate the Hebrew boy babies by throwing them into the Nile. Once again there are people who make important choices. A baby boy is born to a Levite couple. Once again the names are withheld, though later we find out Amram is Moses' father and Jochebed is Moses' mother (see Exod. 6:20). The mother keeps the baby in hiding until he's three months old; at that time she has her daughter, Miriam (we find out her name later, too), place him in a floating basket in the Nile. The Hebrew word *tebah*, translated here for basket, is the same word used in the Genesis 6–9 story for the ark built by Noah: a vehicle for saving life when there is threat from water.

There are a number of ironies evident in the story at this point. The River Nile, instead of being a place of drowning, provides refuge for the baby Moses; it is Pharaoh's daughter who rescues the baby in open defiance of her father's order; Moses' mother is reunited with her child and receives a salary from the government that had intended to kill her son. These ironies would not have happened except for five feisty females who made brave choices: Shiphrah, Puah, Pharaoh's daughter, Miriam, and Jochebed. There are no grandiose plans and no fireworks or trumpets sounding heavenly fanfare. Instead, we watch as a few faithful women resist death and, in doing so, bring forth life. These seemingly inconsequential actions set in motion one of the most significant events in Israel's history—the Exodus of the Hebrew slaves from their captivity in Egypt.

I recently returned from sorting through my parents' belongings in preparation for their relocation to a retirement community.

As is often the case, such tasks become opportunities for learning about our ancestors. We found a certificate from the Brethren Service Committee that was written in December 1942. The certificate acknowledged a small contribution from my grandfather, A. H. Burkholder. The money was to be used for Civilian Public Service "in relieving suffering, in creating good will, and in making Christ known as Prince of Peace." My grandfather signed a statement showing his desire "to support constructive service to humanity." His contribution was "intended as an alternative service to war, in which my [his] conscience does not permit me [him] to engage." (See *The Brethren Encyclopedia* for an article on Civilian Public Service.)

This part of our family story had not been shared with our generation. Had we not discovered the certificate in our farmhouse attic, this part of our family history would have been lost. That's something akin to the names disappearing in the Exodus story. When our stories are not told, we lose something of our identity. When we are silent about our relationship with God over the years, the centrality of our faith is lost. That's what happened with the descendants of Joseph and Jacob. The names disappeared. The stories remained untold. Their identities were lost and their relationship with God was minimized.

It's in this situation that unlikely heroes emerge. The two midwives are God's agents. Miriam, Jochebed, and Pharaoh's daughter also act as a small force against the absolute ruler of an empire. Five individuals, trying to live in ways that promote justice, alter the course of history. Thus begins our Exodus story.

Discussion and Action

1. Listen to a recording of Ken Medema's song "Looking for a Hero." (Check your local library or locate it on Medema's CD entitled *Just One Dance*.) Compare and contrast the ideas expressed there with the themes in the lesson material.

2. Discuss the idea that genocide happens when we don't know the other people's names. Discuss various examples of genocide throughout world history. What were

the causes? Could a few people have made a difference in those situations? Consider viewing a portion of the movie *Schindler's List*. Discuss the statement: "The list is life."

3. Discuss examples of people taking actions of civil disobedience. Talk about your own experiences as appropriate. Recall religious movements that began as an act of civil disobedience. Are there actions of civil disobedience that might be appropriate in our world today? Would group members support one another if such actions were taken?

4. Many denominations are concerned about losing their identity. Talk about your denomination, congregation, or faith tradition. Are there stories, beliefs, or traditions that make you distinctly unique? On what is your identity based? Is your corporate identity being challenged, lost, or preserved? Give specific examples. What are the effects of not telling our story or keeping our name alive?

5. Share about people who have played the role of "midwife" in your life, providing encouragement when something new was being birthed. What common themes do you hear in people's stories?

6. How can you be a midwife in our world today? Where in our world are gutsy women and men needed to stand up to injustice and violence? What witness might your group or congregation make in your local community or the broader world?

7. Conclude your discussion with a few moments of silence. Invite God to guide each person to one thing that needs time, prayer, or action in the coming week. Close in prayer or sing "Heart with loving heart united."

2

God Calls a Leader
Exodus 2:1–3:22

Personal Preparation

1. As you read this session's scripture, be attentive to words, phrases, or themes that move your spirit.
2. Reflect on finding your own identity. Recall the people and events that have helped shape your life. Consider the process of coming to know yourself.
3. Recall a time when you experienced God's powerful presence in your life. Reflect on what God was like in that experience. Take time to savor the experience, thanking God for what you received.
4. Read the session material and background material to learn about call narratives, theophany, and the name Yahweh.

Suggestions for Sharing and Prayer

1. Talk together about the joys, celebrations, losses, and hopes of the past week? Listen prayerfully to everyone who shares, opening your heart to their experiences.
2. Take turns describing the process of finding your personal identity. Notice both common and different experiences of struggle, discomfort, or growth within the group.
3. As a group discuss how each of you came to your various vocations. Were there moments of hesitation or perhaps new direction in these experiences? Recall ways that you became aware of God's call.

4. Discuss portions of this week's scripture that were particularly moving. What questions did you have? Where
   did God speak to you most in these passages?
5. Move into prayer, remembering those concerns mentioned as you gathered. Invite people to pray silently or
   aloud.

Understanding

Our narrative begins at some point "after Moses had grown up,"
yet we find little clarity about his identity. He was raised by
Pharaoh's daughter as an Egyptian prince. In these opening verses, Moses is perceived as an Egyptian by the enslaved Hebrews.
The narrator states that Moses "went out to his people and saw
their forced labor" (Exod. 2:11). He identifies with his Hebrew
heritage and strikes out against the Egyptian oppressor. Moses'
loyalties are clear, but we can only presume that his outward
appearance and adopted family place him in a different camp. In
the midst of this ambiguous identity, Moses assumes the roles of
defender, rescuer, and liberator. Commentator Janzen suggests
that seeking justice for Israel is far more difficult than Moses
had anticipated. "His own people do not willingly accept his
leadership as their liberator" (47).

Part of Moses' developing identity is apparent in how he
responds to situations. We see a growing ability to handle con-
flicts. In 2:12, Moses uses violence to stop an Egyptian from
beating a Hebrew. In the next verses, Moses uses verbal con-
frontation to intervene between two Hebrews. He then flees to
escape the consequences of his previous actions. Later, in the
land of Midian, Moses boldly defends seven women who are
being harassed at the well.

These experiences all hold elements of conflict, violence,
and an imbalance of power. We observe Moses transitioning
from striking out with equal violence to addressing injustice
without violence. Moses is maturing. He stands at the threshold
of a new identity. Indeed, we find that Moses embraces several
new identities within our text. Within two verses (2:21-22), he

becomes a husband, a son-in-law, and a father! Moses has moved from being a fugitive with an uncertain identity to becoming a settled, family man.

God Hears and Remembers

The narrator interrupts Moses' personal story and brings us back to the oppressive circumstances of the Hebrews. The narrator now refers to them as Israelites, a foreshadowing of the people they will become. The language in this retelling emphasizes the depth of the Israelite people's despair. They groan and cry out for deliverance. The repetition and augmentation of language portrays unbearable anguish. Commentators point out that these are not so much prayers or crying out to God as they are simple expressions of pain. A new king has arrived on the scene, and Brueggemann suggests that the Israelites find their collective voice during this new king's reign. A totalitarian regime can keep the oppressed silent for a long time, but now the people experience a turning point. The Hebrew people have become Israelites; they have found the strength necessary to give voice to their suffering. Just as Moses discovers a new identity, his kinfolk also are making an identity shift. They are no longer silent slaves. They are able to speak of their suffering in order to move to a different place.

From our own experiences, we know that talking about our pain and grief is a significant step toward healing. Speaking our truths is a catalyst for change and transformation. Brueggemann notes that this self-assertion is a remarkable matter, for the first task of every marginalized community is to find its voice (706). When the docile silence of slavery is shattered, God hears, notices, and remembers. The Hebrews become Israelites. God is ready to renew a relationship with these people. God will show loyalty to these people whom he has called his own, as evident in 2:24: "God heard their groaning. . . . and took notice of them."

The Hebrew word *yada* in verse 24 is frequently translated as "knew" or "know." The use of this word shows that God is not glancing casually at the situation. There is a deep sense that God understands the Israelite people's suffering and remembers the covenant relationship begun in the book of Genesis. These are not just any suffering people. They are God's people—the people with whom God has entered into holy covenant. God's hearing, remembering, looking, noticing, and knowing indicate that something is about change.

A Call Extended and Resisted

We return to Midian as we resume Moses' story. He has become the settled shepherd and focused family man. In the midst of that pastoral scene, God comes to Moses in the guise of the burning bush. Such visible manifestation of a deity is often referred to as a theophany. Up to this point, God has not taken direct action in this saga. In fact, we have not had any direct words from God until this scene (3:1-22).

A burning bush that does not turn into ashes gets Moses' attention. This impetuous, aggressive person takes time from herding sheep to explore this curious phenomenon. Moses seems more ready to observe and interact, and God sees that Moses is receptive. Claiming a relationship with the oppressed Hebrews, God says, "I am the God of your father, the God of Abraham, the God of Isaac, and the God of Jacob" (3:6). Moses is silent as God outlines plans for delivering the people from their sufferings and bringing them to a bountiful land that flows with milk and honey. Then comes the surprise. God wants Moses to ask Pharaoh to release the people from their bondage! Moses promptly asks: "Who am I that I should go to Pharaoh?"

At this point, Moses hesitates when God calls. The narrator doesn't tell us what is behind Moses' question: "Who am I?" Perhaps Moses felt unworthy. Or perhaps Moses remembered his earlier struggles in not being received very readily as a liberator. He recognizes his own failings through his growing self-knowledge. There's yet another possibility—that after we have had a significant encounter with God, we become afraid of what God might require of us. Whatever the case with Moses, God's response is clear: "I will be with you." God clearly intends for Moses to act as God's empowered agent and avoid relying on his own strength in responding to this call. God promises to lead the way.

May I Ask Who's Calling?

Moses isn't satisfied with knowing God as the God of his ancestors—as important as that is. Moses requests God's name (see 3:13) so that he can tell the Israelites. Perhaps Moses personally wants to know more about God.

Moses displays chutzpah in asking for God's name. He grapples with names and identities, much like you and I do. The answer he receives is a bit mysterious: "I AM WHO I AM." Many commentators suggest a better translation: "I will be who/what I will be." The name also suggests a God who is present within both current and future contexts. The Hebrew word here is often translated *Yahweh*. This is the name of a God who continues mysterious conversation and calls across the ages to those who ponder and take notice.

Discussion and Action

1. Discuss times when you have struggled with identity issues or times when you felt like you were living in two worlds. Discuss living as God's people in the political and cultural "kingdom" of our time.

2. Share information from the research you conducted on the topics of call narratives, the name Yahweh, and theophany.

3. Does God respond to our suffering or our piety? Recall a time when suffering seemed unending for you or another. Were you aware of God's presence at the time? When have you been "remembered" by God when you weren't being particularly prayerful?

4. Consider the early signs of Moses' character. Does he appear to be a good "ministry candidate"? Discuss whether we seek the same characteristics as God does when we seek leaders within the faith community. Whom do we exclude or include? How does your congregation or denomination affirm leadership as a growth process?

5. Discuss whether there would have been an Exodus if the Hebrew slaves had been silent about their oppression. Would there have been a civil rights movement in this

country without the actions of people like Rosa Parks? What does this suggest about our responsibility to give voice to the hurts and injustices of the world today? What in your own life needs to be voiced so you are better able to serve as God's agent in the world?

6. Discuss the significance of Moses receiving God's name. Has there been any change in how you address God? As your relationship with God has grown or changed, what are some names you would ascribe to Yahweh?

7. Talk about resistance you have felt when God called you to a specific ministry or task. How can you support one another when you sense that resistance? In what ways might we test a perceived call?

8. In a phrase or sentence, prayerfully name your calling. Close with a prayer of support for one another and sing together "Here I am, Lord."

3

A Call, a Clash, and a Covenant
Exodus 4:1–6:27

Personal Preparation

1. During the week, read the entire scripture passage and the lesson material. What aspects of the story stand out for you? With what character or aspect of the story do you most identify?
2. Read background material on the term *covenant*, noting the various ways a covenant can be expressed. Pray for the covenants in which you participate, including the relationships within your study group.
3. Listen to a recording of Ken Medema's song "Moses." You can find it on Medema's CD entitled *People of the Sun*. Prayerfully consider the questions asked at the end of the song. If you don't have access to this song, think about the following: To whom or to what are you bound?

Suggestions for Sharing and Prayer

1. Share about times when you have been grateful for God's loving presence in your life. Spontaneously offer a prayer of thanks, using statements of God's faithfulness that have been mentioned by the group.
2. Talk together about times when you have needed affirmation of vocation, focus, or ministry. What got you through those times? How did you experience God in those difficult days?
3. Watch an episode of the television show *Joan of Arcadia*. (Season 1 is available on DVD from Amazon.com, or you can find it in your public library.) Notice how young Joan responds to God's requests. Where do you notice resistance, trust, disappointment,

or acceptance? Note parallels in your own life with Moses' experience in Exodus.
4. As a group discuss ways you might have responded if you were in Moses' situation in today's text. Would you feel confident? What might you say to God? Would you find similar excuses?
5. Pray for openness to learning and growing as you move into studying the lesson.

Understanding

Our scripture lesson begins in the middle of Yahweh's conversation with Moses during this unexpected encounter in the desert. Much of the conversation in 4:1-9 relates to the word *believe.* Moses doesn't think the Hebrews will believe him, so God gives Moses signs to help create belief. Some would say this shows Moses' lack of faith and that whether to believe or not is the main question in this conversation. The Hebrew word here is *aman* from which comes our word "amen." What needs to happen for Moses to say "amen" to God's call? It seems that God has to nudge Moses into belief before Moses can serve as a credible spokesperson whom the Hebrews will believe.

Still Struggling

God's task is not an easy one! Moses raises objection after objection, including a rather passionate plea that he is not eloquent enough for such a responsibility. God answers each concern by giving a sign or miracle. These signs bolster Moses' confidence in God. Throughout the conversation, God remains patient and accommodating. Only in 4:13 do we see anger from God when Moses pleads, "O my Lord, please send someone else." God's anger at Moses does not lead to punishment, however. Instead, God agrees to send Aaron, Moses' brother, to assist in the task of liberation. At each step, God seems willing to accept Moses' questions and fears as legitimate. God clearly desires Moses' trust and is committed to staying close to Moses even when Moses would prefer to distance himself from the entire situation. The success of this mission depends more on God than Moses' eloquence or leadership abilities. God is in charge.

Many of us can identify with Moses and his struggle with God's call. Testing a calling often takes months of praying and seeking discernment within the believing community. We step out in faith when we accept that God is really inviting us to move beyond our comfort zones and do something different. Like Moses, God meets us at our need—patiently walking with us as we move closer to saying "amen" to God's invitation.

Responding to the Message

A number of fast-paced events follow Moses' lengthy conversation with God. Moses leaves his father-in-law's village; God gives final instructions to Moses; Zipporah saves Moses from an attack at night. For purposes of our study, we move on to a brief description of God speaking to Aaron (4:27). Unlike his brother, Aaron readily complies and follows God's instruction to meet Moses in the wilderness. We see no evidence of disbelief, resistance, or struggle. The narrator briefly describes the meeting between Moses and Aaron along with a statement about Moses passing on to Aaron all the words and signs given by Yahweh. Without any mention of traveling from the wilderness or the mountain of God, the narrator transports Moses and Aaron to Egypt where they assemble the oppressed Hebrew slaves. Aaron's quick response to God is matched by the equally immediate response from the Israelite people. They believe the words and signs that Yahweh relays to them. Upon hearing that God has noticed their misery, the Israelites celebrate in worship. Their desperate cries have finally been heard! They respond with heartfelt gratitude. However, the narrator doesn't linger there. After such an extended dialogue between Yahweh and Moses, this whole section seems like a hasty recording of less significant details (4:18-31). It propels us toward the main drama of Moses' encounters with Pharaoh.

Prophets Meet Pharaoh

If Moses and Aaron were on a high after having God's message so overwhelmingly received by the Israelites, these new leaders are now in for a rude awakening when they encounter Pharaoh. We can anticipate Pharaoh's irreverent outburst in 5:2: "Who is the Lord, that I should heed him and let Israel go? I do not know the Lord, and I will not let Israel go." Pharaoh pronounces the Israelites lazy, and, instead of granting the request, Pharaoh orders the unthinkable. They will have to find their own straw for the bricks they must make and still meet their daily quota.

The contest for ultimate authority has begun. Pharaoh's complex machinery of oppression is deployed via the Egyptian taskmasters. When the Israelite supervisors plead with Pharaoh to reconsider his edict, the fearful king continues his unyielding tyranny. The slaves find themselves in an incredibly hopeless situation.

Covenant Expressed

With this increasing burden, Moses turns to God. Interestingly, Moses does not need Aaron's help when conversing with Yahweh. He blames God for the increasing mistreatment of the Israelite people. God acknowledges a long-term connection with the Hebrew people and conveys what this covenant relationship means. Years ago, Yahweh had promised to give Abraham's descendants a special land, and now considering the Israelite slaves and their plight and remembering the covenant, Yahweh has come to free them from bondage. Yahweh is their God and they are Yahweh's people. Janzen notes that this language reflects the Hebrew people's understanding of the familial relationship as portrayed in ancient wedding ceremonies. "The covenant relationship emphasizes God's 'kinship closeness' to this people on whose behalf God will act" (100). God initiated the covenant and will sustain the relationship through acts of deliverance. Despite Yahweh's gracious words of assurance, Moses and the Israelites have a difficult time accepting Yahweh's promises (6:9-12).

The Hebrew experience calls to mind movies such as *Schindler's List, A Beautiful Life,* and *The Pianist.* These movies portray the horrific treatment of the Jewish people during Hitler's regime. The massive military machinery carried out atrocity after atrocity. In the midst of despair, there were unlikely people such as Oskar Schindler (*Schindler's List*), a Nazi party member, womanizer, and war profiteer who saved the lives of more than 1,100 Jews during the Holocaust. A more recent film, *Hotel Rwanda,* portrays genocide on the African continent. Paul Rusesabagina, a hotel manager, saves over 1,200 Tutsi people from being massacred by the Hutu militia. Desperate circumstances often inspire ordinary people to alter their normal routines and make sacrifices as they seek to live justly in a society that is filled with hatred, violence, and inequity.

Moses' story is not over. Perhaps with God's help, the two brothers can still find a way to free the Hebrew slaves.

Discussion and Action

1. Discuss the large and small ways that we as Christians have been called. How do we support people whom God calls—not just ministers, but all of us? What messages do we give one another about our abilities? Do we help each other see ordinary tasks as part of how we live out our calling?

2. Discuss Moses' struggle with God's call. Do you identify with his need for reassurance? Explore the notion that God actually accommodated Moses' needs. Does Moses need to believe before he can be a credible proponent of God's plan?

3. Have you ever felt as if your spirit were breaking? When have you experienced or observed people with broken spirits? How might we support people in such situations?

4. Borrowing language from Exodus 6:26-27, complete the following statement for each person in your group. "The same [*insert a name*] who was [*insert a characteristic such as timid, uncertain*] is the same [*insert the same name*] whom God is calling to [*name a ministry or task*]." Take time to prayerfully consider these statements, using them to affirm God's growing call in your group members.

5. When have you needed to confront a "pharaoh"—someone who burdens or oppresses others? Share stories with the group.

6. Can you acknowledge when you oppress others or cause others to suffer? Though this may be difficult, spend some time in quiet prayer, asking God to reveal when you have displayed behaviors that reflect a pharaoh-like attitude. Consider how you might act upon your insights. Share with the group as you feel led.

7. If group members viewed any of the movies noted in the lesson, compare and contrast key themes with the Exodus story. Where did you see the following themes: suffering, despair, hope, belief, deliverance, or resistance to a task?

8. Recite or sing the African-American spiritual "Go Down Moses." You can get the text from the Internet. It can also be found in many hymnals.

9. Quietly consider what stirred you during the lesson. How might the group pray for you? Close with prayer, naming and praying for spoken and unspoken needs.

4

The Plagues
Exodus 6:28–11:10

Personal Preparation

1. Read the scripture text and lesson material during the week. Notice similarities or differences in God's speech or actions within the accounts of the plagues. Also note Moses' and Pharaoh's speeches and actions, the effects of the plagues, and what the narration is like.
2. Consider your personal allegiances. Who or what do you worship or value? What keeps you from giving your entire allegiance to God?
3. Gather information about agencies that focus on the intersection between faith and the environment. Check with your denomination's website to find projects or task forces that are working at environmental issues.
4. During the week, be aware of situations in which people are oppressed in your community and around the world.

Suggestions for Sharing and Prayer

1. Begin this time together by spending a few minutes in silence, pondering what you would like to share with the group that would build the covenant among you. Consider ways you might be oppressed by unhealthy or destructive patterns of living. Listen with reverence to one another, holding in confidence all that is shared.
2. Talk about circumstances in your own life that once seemed hopeless. How did you feel God's presence in the midst of those circumstances?

3. Talk about experiences from the past week that intersect with the scripture lesson. Where did you notice God moving in those experiences?

4. Describe events or teachings from your early life that shaped your ideas of what God is like. Were those positive or negative experiences? What are the qualities that most helpfully describe the God that you know and experience in your life today?

5. Move into a time of prayer, offering up prayer sentences for needs and concerns among you, as well as joys you wish to celebrate.

Understanding

Polluted water. Frogs. Gnats. Flies. Pestilence. Boils. Hail. Locusts. Dense darkness. Such elements could contribute to the plot of a highly acclaimed horror film! Add opposition to a wily ruler and a nation's struggle for sovereignty and you find yourself in the middle of this week's lesson. Although there is value in taking a detailed look at each plague, for our purposes we will examine some overarching themes. This sizable passage provides continuous drama that escalates each time God exerts great power in the form of a plague.

God vs. Pharaoh

From the outset of this section, we witness a struggle between one who is Sovereign (God) with one who thinks he is sovereign (Pharaoh). The Creator of the universe is pitted against the ruler of the Egyptian empire. Moses and Aaron serve as communicators for the Creator and the Egyptian magicians act as consultants for Pharaoh. The contest is between the God of emancipation and Pharaoh's evil brutality. God's goal is to liberate the Hebrew people.

Pharaoh tries to match Yahweh's power, yet he is wise enough to consult with others. In the first few plagues, we see the magicians matching or imitating the effects of the plagues. But their tricks only go so far. Magic tricks, or technology, are no match for God. Pharaoh has not counted on such tough competition. He does not know Yahweh; he only knows the title "God of the Hebrews." So he may be thinking that this is just another idle idol. He soon discovers that this is a different God and a different kind of power.

Because Pharaoh denies the expansiveness of Yahweh's power, the plagues permeate all levels of Egyptian society. Infestations of flies, gnats, and locusts darken the skies. Such insects are a nuisance, but can you imagine stinking frog corpses covering the ground? It's enough to make you want to croak! Despite the devastating effects of the plagues, Pharaoh refuses to let the Hebrew slaves go into the wilderness to worship God.

Pharaoh clings to the little control he thinks he has. This dynamic is characteristic of people who are addicted to power. At times when the crisis is acute, we get a glimpse of Pharaoh wanting to do something responsible, large-hearted and ultimately healing for all concerned. But when the crisis is over and the impact of the plagues dissipates, he cannot bring himself to honor his commitment by letting the people leave. Thus, the struggle continues. Pharaoh ignores his advisors' counsel. He simply refuses to listen to the very people he has placed in positions of knowledge and insight. In addition, Pharaoh appears unaffected by the suffering that he has brought upon the people of Egypt. As with most power mongers, he cannot see how his behavior is negatively affecting the wellness of other people and the environment. The magicians discover the limits of their power, but Pharaoh cannot acknowledge this for himself. Hence, the plagues continue.

Through this story, we learn that God cares for marginalized people, and God expects those in power to do the same. Yahweh, the God of creation and covenant, wants both the powerful and the vulnerable to genuinely respect and care for one another. Misusing power in any way, as Pharaoh does, is contrary to the witness of the scriptures. God often turns the tables on those who take advantage of the poor and vulnerable. For instance, the first chapters of Luke's Gospel include Mary's song declaring how God has brought down the proud and lifted up the poor (Luke 1:46-55), Jesus' proclamation that he has been sent to release those who are captive (Luke 4:16-21), and Jesus' teachings about circumstance reversals (Luke 6:20-26).

A Hardened Heart

We cannot study the plagues without noticing the language that describes Pharaoh and the hardening of his heart. The biblical witness refers both to Yahweh hardening Pharaoh's heart and to the hard heart being the result of Pharaoh's own volition. How are we to understand this? Does Yahweh deliberately control Pharaoh so he doesn't have a change of heart? Does Yahweh make the Egyptians suffer through these incredibly devastating plagues by hardening Pharaoh's heart?

Walter Brueggemann addresses this issue by suggesting that fate and choice are juxtaposed within Pharaoh's actions. "He is, indeed, fated by Yahweh to fail, but he also chooses his own destruction in a series of choices" (764). Pharaoh can be viewed as both victim and perpetrator of his own destruction. God's intention is to be victorious in this conflict with Pharaoh. God also gives Pharaoh many opportunities to make choices that will bring about restoration; however, Pharaoh's need for power gets in his way. Brueggemann also warns us to avoid trying to tame this wild and elusive Yahweh whom we can only begin to understand. Even in the Book of Job, God reminds Job that human minds cannot understand everything about God's ways (Job 38–40).

God's Intentions

Although we are left with several questions, there is one thing that cannot be questioned: God's desire to be in relationship with the Hebrew people. God wants them to know the One who acts with a mighty hand. The One who turns the Nile's water into blood is the same Yahweh who wants to know and be known. God will restore a relationship with the Hebrews and they will be free to worship God. Indeed, Yahweh has responded to the cries of the covenant people. Yahweh was the God of Abraham and Sarah and is the God of these people and every person who cries out for release from suffering.

The people who had forgotten their own names have been reintroduced to God, now known as Yahweh. Knowing Yahweh, they will come to know themselves. Though the Hebrew people are completely silent in these plague narratives, they surely have been observing Yahweh's work on their behalf. They have watched the Egyptian people suffer as the plagues brought death and despair throughout the land. Although once captives, the Hebrew people are now free. God's hand has reached into their world and drawn them into a protective and loving embrace. God brings forth this people to fulfill the covenant made with Abraham and Sarah long ago. God wants to be known and revered. God also wants to serve as the Israelite people's king.

Discussion and Action

1. Discuss examples of when the relationship between Creator and creature has been distorted. Identify examples in our contemporary life when power is misused and the well-being of people and planet are at risk. Share information from agencies that work at making connections between faith and the environment. How might your group address these issues in your community?

2. When have you struggled with God? Where have you seen others struggle to maintain their power when everything around them is crumbling? What does it take for such a person to acknowledge their limits of power and find health?

3. The lesson material highlights Yahweh, who shows deep compassion for the marginalized. How might our lives and faith reflect that same attitude? What tables need to be turned in our world? Who is excluded from fully participating in our faith communities? Who has difficulty accessing adequate resources for living?

4. Discuss the nature of God in the plague narratives. Are there different characteristics or images here than in other scriptures passages?

5. What is your response to Pharaoh's hardheartedness? Have you ever experienced a hardened heart? What

contributed to such constricted compassion? How are we, like Pharaoh, unwilling to change when we hear a message from God?

6. Close with prayer or sing a hymn that focuses on God's presence and healing. Examples include the well-known spiritual "Precious Lord, take my hand" or "In the rifted Rock I'm resting."

5

From Passover to Praise
Exodus 12:1–15:21

Personal Preparation

1. Pray for wisdom and understanding as you read the scripture text for this week and prepare for this session. Be attentive to various literary devices in the scripture text: instructions for ritual celebration or worship, dialogue between main characters, narration of the story, poetic response, etc.

2. Recall rituals or ordinances of the church that have been particularly meaningful to you. Examples include anointing, communion, love feast, baptism, and confession. How have those events helped nurture your relationship with God? Give thanks to God, savoring how God was real to you in those moments.

Suggestions for Sharing and Prayer

1. Think of symbols or words that tie you to the wider story of faith and God's promises. Examples might include a cross, fire, fish, Bible, peace sign, intertwined circles, dove. What do you think about when you see these symbols? Group members might differ greatly in the feelings and memories associated with these things.

2. Talk together about specific rituals or ordinances of the church that have been particularly significant in either positive or negative ways. Which of these do you want to perpetuate? eliminate?

3. Facilitate discussion about what it means to experience "a yoke of oppression." Have group members experienced something like this in their spiritual lives? What is it like to have such a burden lifted? If someone in the group feels spiritually burdened in this way, take time to listen, talk, and pray.
4. Pray for guidance as you spend time together, seeking to better understand this story.

Understanding

In this week's scripture passage, the Hebrew people transition from their forced allegiance to an Egyptian master's edicts to allegiance to Yahweh, the Creator of the universe.

A Faith Record

In this part of the Exodus story, liturgical remembrance is embedded within the historical narrative. These passages are woven together without distinguishing between actual reporting of the event and God's instructions for remembering the Passover event through ritual celebration. The central concern is that people in future generations, especially children, should have a sense of participating in this great liberation brought about by God. Yahweh freed the people from bondage and guided them to the Promised Land. This record of faith informed and formed the fledgling Israelite community.

Perhaps we can best understand this by looking at a ritual common in my faith tradition. In the Church of the Brethren we observe something called love feast. Our spiritual ancestors understood the value of attending to the actions shown by Jesus at the Passover supper with his disciples. During love feast, we wash one another's feet, eat and break bread together. We are not merely replicating Jesus' actions. We are actively living out the events in that upper room. When we come to the Eucharist, we say, "This *is* the communion of the body of Christ." This stands in contrast to some other faith traditions who say, "This *was* the communion of the body of Christ." The ancient story becomes our story and we become part of the ancient story that continues even today!

In this lesson's scripture, the narrator invites us to remember the Passover event within the context of the total Exodus experience and the people's responses to God's intervention. The Israelites claim their name and identity while forming a new allegiance with God, who leads them. They obediently participate in the event and remember the details by re-enacting portions of the event annually. Through this, they participate in the covenant with Yahweh.

Bread to Go

The Israelites are sometimes referred to as "people of marked doors" and "people of the hurried bread." God tells the Israelite slaves to mark their doorposts with blood from the lambs they had slaughtered for their final meal in Egypt. These marks are not for God's benefit. God already knows where each slave family lives! The marked doorposts become a public sign of who is exempt from destruction. God's promise and protection are present and real. In the darkness of nighttime crisis, the Israelites are people of marked doors—people who claim the deliverance of God.

Regarding the reference to "people of the hurried bread," waiting for bread to rise was not an option for people escaping at a moment's notice. Unleavened bread, or hurried bread, provides sustenance and serves as a reminder of the situation's urgency as the Israelites celebrated rituals of remembrance in the years that followed. This was not a leisurely meal; they didn't have all the time in the world. God calls the people to liberation through obedience.

God Triumphs

Finally, we see the proverbial light at the end of the tunnel. At last, Yahweh is triumphant! We first see a victory over Pharaoh's hardened heart. The Egyptian ruler implores the Israelites to "Rise up, go away from my people. . . . Go, worship the Lord, as you said. . . . And bring a blessing on me, too!" (12:31-32).

Pharaoh acknowledges that he can no longer force the people to serve him. God is their master now. Later, in Exodus 14, Pharaoh considers the economic ramifications of his decision and tries to reclaim the Hebrews as slaves, but God will not allow this covenant people to be reinstated into slavery. God triumphs over the whole Egyptian army who also acknowledges God's mighty power.

We cannot speak of God's triumph without noting that Yahweh has also won the hearts of the Israelite people. Yahweh is their deliverer. Miriam's song (15:21) and the song of Moses (15:1-18) overflow with praise for the Master of creation who used wind and water to overcome those who harmed God's people. These songs flow out of gratefulness for God's attentive care and provision. God's actions have shown them that Moses' words were true: "Do not be afraid, stand firm, and see the deliverance that the LORD will accomplish for you today; for the Egyptians whom you see today you shall never see again. The Lord will fight for you, and you have only to keep still" (Exod. 14:13-14).

We must acknowledge here that this image of a triumphant, warrior God who kills Israel's oppressor is an image that may be difficult to accept. In fact, we may find it offensive. Yet the language is there and it is part of our faith story. How are we to understand this story and these actions of God? We can only touch lightly on this issue in this study, but perhaps a few observations may be helpful.

The story itself witnesses to a situation that seemingly cannot be resolved by the Israelites themselves. They have no power, no leverage, and no way to accomplish liberation from their oppressors. If it was to be done, God had to do for the Hebrews what they could not do for themselves. A culture that oppresses people must either be changed or dismantled if those who are enslaved by it are to be truly liberated. Through the plagues, we saw that Pharaoh would not change even though there were multiple opportunities to make different choices. It is clear from the story that societies that flourish by oppressing some of its people are not what God intends. Pharaoh and his army suffered the consequences of continuing to make choices that robbed the Hebrews of life. God's overriding intention was for the Hebrews' oppression to be ended. And God went about the business of overturning the oppressor. We should avoid the temptation to dismiss these uncomfortable images or try to tame this part of God. Even in the Gospels, we find struggle for power and authority. Likewise, such tensions are rampant in our world today.

And so Israel's freedom is bought at a great price. God instructs the Israelites to remember what happened in its totality. God wants the people to remember who they are as a people who were once enslaved but were miraculously freed. In Exodus 13:8, the people are told to tell their children: "It is because of what the Lord did for me when I came out of Egypt." They are invited, as are we, to remember their redemption and to keep the memories alive. God wants us to tell the stories, both painful and pleasant, so we can stand witness to God's action and presence in our lives.

Discussion and Action

1. Choose one or two rituals or events that are central to your congregation or denomination. How does it contribute to forming your identity as a people? Can you maintain your identity without it?

2. Sometimes we only recall significant stories of church life when we celebrate significant anniversaries. What stories might be helpful to tell on a more regular basis to help remember the faith events that shaped your congregation?

3. Over the next three sessions of sharing and prayer time, plan for participants to share their own stories of being liberated by God. Each person should be prepared to share for approximately fifteen minutes, depending upon the size of your group. Such an activity will deepen your relationships and move the group to a new level of sharing. Decide who will share their faith journey next week. Support, encourage, and accept that some people may want to pass on this opportunity.

4. Discuss the image of God as warrior portrayed in the Old Testament. How does this image fit with your understanding of God? As people of peace, how do we internalize this part of the story? In what ways is this image perpetuated today?

5. Discuss the idea that oppressive systems must either be changed or dismantled if those enslaved by them are to find liberation. As we move toward God's life-giving future, what systems must be dismantled or changed? How might we respond when political voices speak of a culture of life while creating a culture of death by waging war and destroying creation?

6. Invite a time of quiet reflection, allowing the things that touched you to plant a seed in your spirits. Close by reciting the prayer adapted from a traditional Navajo blessing:

My feet go before me.
My hands go before me.
My heart goes before me.

May my feet bring peace.
May my hands bring peace.
May my heart bring peace.

There is peace all around me.
Peace . . . Peace . . . Peace.

6

Wilderness Wanderings
Exodus 15:22–18:27

Personal Preparation

1. Pray for a spirit open to God's leading as you read the scripture and lesson material this week. Notice the honest account of God's people in the wilderness.
2. Read background material on the wilderness or other related material such as Waldemar Janzen's essay on "Plagues, Signs and Wonders" in his *Exodus* commentary (pp. 454-55). How does this material help you understand the events in our scripture?
3. Take time during the week to ponder any "wilderness" times in your life. How did you experience God in those times? Did anything new come out of that time?
4. During your prayer time, invite God to give you a trusting spirit. Find a favorite hymn or scripture song that seeks/promises increased faith during uncertainty and use the lyrics as a prayer.

Suggestions for Sharing and Prayer

1. As a group, consider this scenario: You are anticipating a group trip to a place that none of you has ever been. Your travel agent has communicated with you exclusively through e-mail. The agent promises to serve as your tour guide and guarantees that you will love the destination, sight unseen. What questions might you have? Would you agree to such a trip? How might you

feel about paying a hefty deposit? Consider the Israelites
and their experiences regarding the land God had promised them.
2. Share from your lives during the past week. In what
ways have you experienced God's provision? Where
have you wondered if God was present? Hold each person and their sharing in reverence.
3. If you found meaningful hymn texts or scriptures in your
preparation for the class, share them with the group.
4. Have the selected people share their personal faith stories (at least fifteen minutes each). Pray briefly for each
person after they tell about their journey. Thank God for
the blessing of each person and ask for continued guidance on the journey ahead. Decide who will share their
faith stories the next time you meet. Again, be sensitive
to those individuals who might not be ready or willing to
share.
5. Close this time with prayer in response to the needs of
individual group members by naming each person and
offering specific prayers, repeating in unison: "Give us
this day our daily bread." Conclude with the Lord's
Prayer.

Understanding

The Israelites, delivered from horrific oppression in Egypt, go
along for a little while, grateful for all God has done for them.
Then they hit some bumps in the road. The people complain
about their circumstances. They become anxious about their
future and question their leaders. The group's collective memory of the past is much rosier than the actual events. The Israelite
people quickly forget that God has provided for them in the past
and has promised to take care of them always. Does this sound
like some congregations that you know?

An Honest Portrayal

Our scripture lesson reports a series of encounters between
Israel, Moses, and God. The narrator gives us an honest portrayal

of attitudes and behaviors of the people, who are struggling to live in stressful circumstances. Just like us, the Israelites were trying to understand God's intentions for their lives. They are not a perfect people—far from it! The name of one of the places they stop on their journey describes the nature of the people and what happened there. In Exodus 17:7, Moses names the place after he feels his life is in danger from the angry congregation. Moses calls the place *Massah* (test) and *Meribah* (quarrel) because the Israelites ask: "Is the Lord among us or not?" It seems that one name is not enough to describe these testy and quarrelsome people! It takes two names to say it all.

God's people, then and now, can be testy and quarrelsome, as well as loving and faith-filled. The ancient writer's honesty reminds us to speak the truth about our own lives. Too often we have covered up the truth of our struggles with each other, only to have them emerge later in explosive conflict. And sometimes we cover up our struggles with questions about God. In both cases we miss the opportunity for growth and wellness with the One who says: ". . . for I am the Lord who heals you" (Exod. 15:26). Yahweh helps us find healing as we acknowledge our pain.

In the months of writing these lessons, I found myself reflecting on my experience with my mother as she fought a losing battle with Alzheimer's disease and other health conditions. Her memorial service offered an opportunity for me (and her pastors) to share about her life. I would not have been truthful had I not acknowledged her struggle with anger over the years; she was as testy as those ancient Israelites. Yet that is not the whole story. She was also a generous person and dedicated Sunday school teacher who was committed to God and the church. Acknowledging the painful aspects of being my mother's daughter has brought healing and helped me to understand the positive influences she had in my life and the lives of those around her. I believe we find healing when we face the harder issues that affect our faith communities.

A journey in the wilderness invites us to self-examination and honest confession. The Gospels record that Jesus went into the wilderness after his baptism and faced temptations in that setting. These experiences in the desert helped Jesus clarify his relationship with God and shaped his ministry. Church history also includes stories of medieval mystics whose wilderness experiences led to spiritual illumination. The wilderness has usually been portrayed as an arena for struggling with temptation as well as a place of refuge with God. This was the case for the ancient Israelites as well.

God the Provider
Despite the testy and quarrelsome nature of God's people, God keeps providing! The Exodus narrative does not give a detailed, historical account of every single moment of Israel's wilderness journey. Instead, this story highlights some of the Israelites' encounters with God, particularly those in which God gives a sign. This is a document that invites us to reflect theologically— to notice what God is like, how God responds, and what all of this means for our faith.

When the Israelites come to the place called Marah and find only bitter, undrinkable water, God provides a piece of wood for Moses to toss into the water. Immediately, the water becomes sweet and drinkable (Exod. 15:22-26). Within a few verses, the people arrive at Elim, where it seems there is refreshment and shade for the weary, wilderness-worn people (Exod. 15:27). In Exodus 16, God provides both bread and meat for the people when they cry out in hunger and frustration. These staples are not a one-time sign, but an ongoing, daily provision on the long journey. Within this story, we also find the provision of rest in the form of the sabbath. God provides a time to pause from the journey. The people stop gathering food for one day and simply rest. And in response to another plea for water, God uses Moses' staff to quench the people's thirst (Exod. 17:1-7).

In all of these instances, God graciously provides what the people need, what they cannot provide for themselves. In these encounters, the people begin to learn the lessons of trusting in Yahweh.

Notice that the Israelites are not totally inactive in Exodus 16. They must exert some personal energy to collect the manna and catch the quail. Though God provides, the Holy One expects that we recognize and become active participants in the process. Human actions do not make manna appear—that's all grace—but it is human responsibility to receive it, use it wisely, and refrain from hoarding. We are also expected to trust that God will provide for the next day.

God's works and loving guidance are woven into these stories. God responds to the people's needs consistently. Through the wilderness wanderings, the people learn about the nature of God. The God who seemed distant while they were enslaved in Egypt is now being revealed to them at every point along their journey.

Welcome, Worship, and Wisdom

In contrast to the previous scenes of complaining sojourners and fighting enemies, Exodus 18 offers a homey, familial atmosphere. We can almost hear an audible sigh of relief. Moses has arrived at the mountain of God (Exod. 18:5). Afterwards, he is surprised by a visit from his beloved family—his wife, sons, and father-in-law. There are no tensions evident here between son-in-law and father-in-law. Moses welcomes this contingent with reverent bowing and kissing. They talk about each other's welfare, share deeply from the wells of their life experiences, and rejoice in the blessings they have received. The chapter continues with worship and eating together. As Moses shifts to his leadership responsibilities, Jethro advises his son-in-law about a better way to care for the administrative and judicial needs of the growing community.

This passage offers a number of interesting dynamics. Moses' family relationships provide striking contrast to the scheming, strained family relationships portrayed in the Book of Genesis. Do you recall the rivalries embedded in the stories of Cain and Abel, Jacob and Esau, Joseph and his brothers, as well as Rachel and Leah? Here in Exodus 18, in-law relationships are peaceful and wisdom from an elder is welcomed. There is also the question of whether Jethro is already a worshiper of Yahweh or not. The passage could be interpreted either way. In any case, Jethro is an outsider to the Israelite community. Yet he is welcomed readily and participates fully in corporate rituals of worship.

As this lesson concludes, God's people are experiencing a brief respite from their journey. They have not reached their intended destination, but they are developing a new identity as a community of God's people. As they pause along the way, they take time for remembering the story of God's deliverance. They participate in corporate celebration and worship. They now see themselves as part of God's beloved and emerging family!

Discussion and Action

1. Discuss when you haven't recognized God's provisions in your life. When has longing for the familiar "good old days" kept you from seeing God's provision? When have you needed someone else to help you recognize God's faithfulness?

2. Read Psalm 78, particularly verses 18-20. Notice how the psalmist speaks about the time in the wilderness and the questions raised about God. What questions have you had about God in your wilderness times?

3. Do we really pray for "daily bread," or do we demand a five-course meal? Consider limiting your food intake for a number of days this week, being mindful of what it is like to eat only what you need.

4. Talk together about times when you have paused on your journey for celebration or reflection. In what ways do you balance activity and rest, work and sabbath? How does your congregation honor the need for sabbath for your pastor/s or other staff?

5. Discuss Jethro's role in the Exodus story. When do we encourage newcomers to provide leadership and share wisdom within our congregations? What do we require

before inviting someone to serve in that capacity? How are the wisdom, gifts, and leadership of elders honored and used in the church?

6. Sing or read the refrain of "Great is thy faithfulness," found in most hymnals. In what ways have you received mercies or provisions from God "morning by morning"? In a word, phrase, or brief sentence, share the mercies that came to mind. Close with prayer.

7

The Law and the Covenant
Exodus 19–24

Personal Preparation

1. As you read the scripture and lesson material, pray that you might better understand the God of Exodus—the One who liberates and covenants with Israel and with us. How do you experience God in this scripture passage?
2. Review what you learned in your research for previous lessons about the terms *theophany* and *covenant*. What do these words mean? How do they help us understand the relationship between God and the Israelite people? Consider how they connect with this week's lesson.
3. Spend some time in quiet reflection. Recall the times when you felt closest to God. Can you describe what God was like? Or was it beyond description? What was your response to God? How were you changed?

Suggestions for Sharing and Prayer

1. Talk about significant happenings, celebrations, and changes that have occurred in the past week. Be aware of things for inclusion in prayer.
2. Listen as the designated people share their faith stories (fifteen minutes each). Thank God for each person after they share. Pray about specific situations as led. Decide who will share about their faith journey at your next meeting.

3. Discuss ways that the Ten Commandments have been part of your life. Share significant understandings with the group.

4. As you conclude the sharing time, pray together about the needs or joys mentioned by the group. Close this time by singing "Lord, listen to your children,"or read Psalm 5:1-3.

Understanding

As we begin this section at Mt. Sinai, we recall Yahweh's demanding words to Pharaoh: "Let my people go, so that they may worship me in the wilderness" (Exod. 7:16). The dramatic flight from Egypt signifies bringing the Israelite people closer to God. The people of Israel were freed *from* slavery. However, they were freed *for* establishing a relationship with God, thus giving them a particular identity as a people. Previously they were in a forced relationship with Pharaoh. Now they are in a bonded relationship, borne out of God's compassion. This is a situation where the people can choose whether to commit to, sustain, and maintain the relationship. The choice is theirs.

Worship and Covenant-Making

In Exodus 19, the very Creator of the universe fills the atmosphere with an awesome and utterly holy presence. Heaven and earth converge in this place. At the foot of Mt. Sinai, the Israelite people are given a new identity as Yahweh's treasured people. They become a priestly kingdom and a holy nation (Exod. 19:6). God's actions inspire awe. Commentator Walter Brueggemann suggests that the worship experience at Mt. Sinai transforms the Israelites as individuals and as a gathered community (837). The people are released from their former identity as a wandering band of slaves and transformed into a nation. They embrace this new identity by saying, "Everything that the Lord has spoken we will do" (Exod. 19:8).

We must not trivialize this close encounter with God. We can understand how it transformed the Israelite people by looking at our own experiences with God. My experience as a spiritual director informs me in this area. I have observed people on retreat who met God in such a powerful, healing way that they found freedom, courage, and a new sense of self. Indeed, they were transformed! Their retreat experience was so powerful that they were connected to God in a new way. In that kind of circumstance, people were willing to say, "Everything God has spoken we will do." Like the Israelites at Mt. Sinai, they made a covenant with God.

Theophany (an experience of God's powerful presence) and covenant-making go together in this text and in life. God's word is heard. God's presence permeates our lives and we respond as people who have been transformed. The Hebrew people initiated their metamorphosis as they fled from Pharaoh's clutches in Egypt. Israel made a decision for complete obedience. The people willingly embraced a new identity and new life. For the Israelites, becoming a nation was a process. They began to understand God's nature as they walked across the wilderness, eating the food and drinking the water provided by the One leading them. The transformation continues as the people join together in worship and commitment to God.

What does this mean for us as Christians? Many denominations gather annually as a whole body at a convention site to vote on policies and make important decisions on behalf of the community of faith. Such actions surely shape and define who we are. But there is more. We also worship together during these events and sometimes we are touched so deeply by the Holy One that we are never the same. And in all of that we are shaped and defined.

And Now Comes the Law
Israel has agreed to become a holy nation and a priestly kingdom. How will they accomplish such a goal? What does this really mean for the people as individuals? How are they to live as this type of community? Immediately after making the covenant, God provides ten principles for living together in positive ways, otherwise known as the Ten Commandments (Exod. 20:1-17).

Traditionally, the Ten Commandments have been divided into two tablets: those laws concerning relationship with God and those laws concerning relationship with our neighbors. We must understand our relationship with God in order to understand our relationship with neighbors. And the way we respond to God's call in our lives affects the way we truly "see" our neighbors.

As God reminds the Israelites to care for the sojourner, we begin to see evidence of the Israelites developing an eye for "the other." Why? Because God helped them when they were sojourners in Egypt. As we examine God's commandments and rules described in chapters 21–24, we are aware that God is designing a community with non-exploitative social relationships. This band of erstwhile former slaves becomes a social model for living together in a new way. Indeed, the Law given by God articulates a clear principle against every kind of exploitative social relationship and promotes a vision of humans living together in transforming and liberating ways.

The Sabbath

Though we don't have space in this study to examine each of the commands in Exodus 20, we will explore God's command to remember the sabbath and keep it holy. When we remember the sabbath, we honor the Creator by resting. God needed rest from the work of creation in Genesis 1, and those made in God's image also need rest and refreshment.

It is significant that the entire community is expected to rest. Everyone is included—men, women, children, slaves of both genders, resident aliens in the towns, and even the animals! God declares a wholesale work stoppage. These people are no longer forced to labor continuously as slaves are required to do. They have been freed from compulsory work to rest like their Creator.

We may not have compulsory work as the Hebrew slaves in ancient Egypt, but we do have our compulsions as a society and individuals. Often we are our own taskmasters, driving ourselves to the type of weariness that does not disappear with one or two days off each week. Such a driven lifestyle takes a toll on our spiritual, physical, and emotional health. Can we say we are free? Or are we still in bondage? God's invitation to remember and keep the sabbath is countercultural; it resists the economic system of our time that tells us to work more so we can buy more. However, if we are in bondage to the dominant economic system to which we readily pay homage, we will not have true healing of our lives. True liberation and healing come in reclaiming our loyalty to the One who rested on the seventh day and invites us to do the same.

Discussion and Action

1. Discuss what it means that God's people in Exodus were called to become a holy nation and a priestly kingdom. How might God's leadership be similar to or different from other nations with human kings? Do we really have a distinct identity as Christians? If so, in what ways is that identity lived out? If not, with what group or groups do you identify?

2. Discuss the suggestion in the lesson that the way we attend to God determines the way we attend to our neighbor and vice versa.

3. Why do you think God made so many rules? What was their purpose? How do the laws recorded in Exodus empower people to develop non-exploitative relationships? Where do you notice people of faith modeling such behavior? Where do we fail? How might your group or congregation be intentional about proclaiming and modeling non-exploitative relationships? If you were beginning a new church community, how might you shape it?

4. How does your church address the command regarding not killing? Examples for discussion might include capital punishment, war, abortion, or euthanasia. Discuss other ways that life is killed or devalued slowly, in unacknowledged and unnoticed ways.

5. What are the ways that you plan for sabbath in your life? Share ideas with the group. How might you support one another in finding sabbath?

6. The Ten Commandments require "translation" into our contemporary context. Discuss how we might understand these laws as guiding us toward abundant lives, a promised way of living where there is enough for everyone and no one is exploited. What needs to change in our lives for true abundant living to become a reality?

7. Close by reciting as your prayer the words of the Harry Emerson Fosdick hymn "O God, in restless living" (found in many hymnals or by searching the web).

8

Details, Details, Details!
Exodus 25–31

Personal Preparation

1. As you read the scripture texts for this week, notice the attention to detailed instructions regarding worship space and ritual. Ponder what witness these details give the faith community then and now.
2. Do some background reading on the terms *sanctuary, tabernacle,* and *ark of the covenant.* Notice how these words are used in the biblical text.
3. Read the essays on "Consecration" (pp. 437-38) and "Beauty" (pp. 436-37) in Janzen's *Exodus* commentary.
4. Take time during the week to mentally or physically walk through your church building. Where are the most holy or sacred places? Do you experience a sense of "beauty" in the building?

Suggestions for Sharing and Prayer

1. Talk about the events of the past week. In what ways have you seen God at work?
2. Ask the designated individuals to share their faith stories. Say a prayer of thanks for God's work in each person's life. If there is anyone else who has not had a chance to share his or her faith story and wishes to do so, plan for this at the next session.
3. Encourage group members to share ways they make a place for God in their busy lives. Talk about the ways

you give priority to building a relationship with God. This may be helpful for those who struggle in this effort.
4. Discuss what makes a place holy. Do some places seem holier than others? What helps you experience holiness, awe, or beauty in your church? Take a tour of your church building. Where are the holy places? Are they the same for everyone?
5. What objects does your congregation consider holy or set apart for worshipful purposes only? Are there any prohibitions regarding use of those items? What does this say about how we understand holiness?
6. Pray for those who are designers, builders, construction workers, artists, worship team members, and other creative people in your congregation or in the wider church community. Pray for openness to see how God works through them to create an environment conducive to worship.

Understanding

While preparing this lesson, I shared with a colleague some of my frustrations with the many details in this lesson's scripture passages. This wise sister reminded me that beginners often need detailed instructions, while experienced students need fewer details because they understand the basics. With beginners, however, one should avoid taking anything for granted.

So it was with the Israelite community. They were beginners at being a covenant people. They received the Law (the Ten Commandments) and made a solemn promise to be obedient. Now what? They need detailed instruction on living out this covenant, particularly in establishing community worship. With a multitude of detail describing the physical preparations needed for the community's worship life, instructions are given for making and maintaining the tabernacle, ritual garb for priestly leaders, specifications for sacrifices, consecration of leaders, and keeping the sabbath. The list appears endless. For our purposes, we will look at some of the broader categories.

Taking an Offering

God initiates the process for giving offerings, a necessity if there are to be resources for the building projects that God has in mind. God does not coerce, threaten, or intimidate people to donate. Interestingly, God invites a voluntary response, saying the offering is to be taken "from all whose hearts prompt them to give . . ." (Exod. 25:2). What a contrast to the life of slavery. What freedom to give from the heart!

We are reminded that with God there is free will; we can choose how to respond to God. Generosity is impossible if the collected offering is forced. Yahweh's relationship with the Israelites promotes a spiritual freedom that invites us to do great things for God.

Making a Space for God

Sanctuary and *tabernacle* are two terms used in our text to refer to what God wants built. *Sanctuary* is the broader term meaning "holy" or "hallow." It signifies a place set apart for God. In modern language, sanctuary has come to mean a place of worship. The term *tabernacle* refers to a "dwelling place." It is akin to a tent dwelling, instead of a house. The tabernacle is not meant to be permanent. Instead the verbal blueprint calls for something portable that can be carried on a journey. In this case, the tabernacle is designed to carry a box or "ark." The ark houses the actual covenant agreement between God and the Israelite people. This agreement has been written on the two tablets of the Law. From the dimensions given, the ark of the covenant is approximately three-fourths the size of a spinet piano.

In the construction of these items, portability is important. We have already seen God's presence in the pillar of cloud and pillar of fire. God is not a God of one place or time. Unlike many of the deities prominent during that time period, God is not tied to one holy place. God is still on the move, guiding the people. God's presence can be experienced and known anywhere. God is leading the Israelite people on this journey to the Promised Land.

Attending to Details and Beauty

Some people say that "the devil is in the details." In Exodus 25–31, God is in the details! Skillful work is required in the building, sewing, and worship preparation. Precious gems, fine fabrics, and valuable wood are used in the worship of God. To people committed to simple living, these preparations sound quite extravagant. Simple and functional—that's all we need, right? According to the Old Testament perspective, beauty contributes to the creation and restoration of life's wholeness (shalom). Conversely, everything disruptive of shalom robs life of beauty.

Throughout my years in ministry I have planned numerous worship experiences that were held in places not typically used for worship. Four unadorned walls with people sitting in metal folding chairs is not very conducive to a worshipful atmosphere. In those settings, it has been important to draw people in through their senses—to otherwise create a setting that invites people into communion with God, who is the ultimate source of all beauty.

Consecrating Leaders

In living out the covenant with Yahweh, the Israelites also needed leaders for their worship life together. Exodus 28 gives extensive instruction regarding priestly garb. From underwear to turban, priestly attire is described in great detail.

God does not stop with vestments, but moves on to describe the consecration of these leaders (Exod. 29:1-46). Aaron and his descendants are set apart to oversee the Israelites' worship life. This is not a seven-minute service of ordination, but seven *days* of celebration involving sacrifices, anointing with oil, and dabbing the priests with blood on various parts of their bodies. It sounds pretty messy! Yet the extensive instructions and attention to detail emphasize the complete dedication required of people in leadership in the life of this faith community.

Keeping the Sabbath

Exodus 31 concludes with the reiteration of God's commands regarding the sabbath. There is the connection with resting and

God's creation of the world. But there's something more here. Resting on the sabbath and focusing on God symbolize keeping the covenant. What other deity invites people to take the day off? Exodus 31 goes on to say that dishonoring the covenant is punishable by death. This sounds harsh, but there is the sense that keeping the sabbath is so crucial to life with God that not observing the sabbath invites death. We know God through our work, ministry, and rituals; we also know God through reflection and rest. For a people who was once enslaved, the relationship with this new Master is a gift to be celebrated.

Discussion and Action

1. What significance do you draw from the fact that the tabernacle is portable? What might this tell us about God? about worship?

2. Discuss how your congregation approaches stewardship. Talk about the idea that true giving is impossible when people are forced to give.

3. How does your congregation use the senses of taste, smell, touch, sight, and hearing to experience God? How does your congregation approach the issue of having an aesthetically pleasing worship space and building? For those of us who worship in simple meetinghouses, how do we receive the notion that God desires things of beauty in the holy place? Discuss ways to enhance worship in your congregation.

4. How does your congregation call out the gifts of people who can build up the church? How do we set people apart for holy vocations or tasks? Who in your congregation contributes regularly to the worship experience? You might be surprised at all the many ways that people are involved.

5. Consider how this passage might be received in other settings and cultures. What do instructions about precious gems and the finest materials say to people in abject poverty? Is it right to build elaborately decorated houses of worship when there is such suffering and poverty in the world?

6. What are your practices or rituals for commissioning or blessing people for tasks such as ministry, Christian education, work camp experiences, disaster response, church board leadership, volunteer service, etc.

7. Talk about your perspectives on vestments for pastoral leaders. What significance do vestments have for you? How does this relate to the simple and plain dress of some religious traditions? What does this mean in regard to one's understanding of the "priesthood of all believers"?

8. Close with prayer. Highlight key concepts that emerged from the study. Invite God to lead and guide group members throughout the coming week.

9

A Calf Crisis and Covenant Continuity
Exodus 32–34

Personal Preparation

1 Pray for a spirit of discernment as you prepare for this week's lesson.
2. Spend some time praying with Exodus 34:6-7, noticing how God's nature is described in this poetry. Be attentive to how you are responding to God as described here. When have you experienced these qualities in God?
3. In a Bible dictionary, investigate the meaning of the words *merciful, gracious, steadfast love, faithfulness,* and *apostasy.* Read the essays on "Covenant" in Janzen's Exodus commentary (pp. 438-41) or in Eugene Roop's Believers Church commentary on *Rom.* (pp. 315-16).

Suggestions for Sharing and Prayer

1. Spend some time talking about when you have felt God's presence or absence in your life during the past week. Compare your feelings with what young children experience as separation anxiety. How do we respond emotionally when we feel vulnerable or insecure?

2. Discuss where you find assurance of God's presence for your daily walk? What gives you assurance of divine presence?
3. As a group, talk about experiences when your faith in God has been challenged. Was it restored? Invite deep sharing.
4. As Christians, we have distinct qualities in our faith life that have set us apart from others. What does that distinctiveness mean to you? What are your personal "distinctives"?
5. Spend some time in silent prayer for individuals in your group. Invite God's Spirit to guide your time together.

Understanding

What a difference forty days make! The Israelites moved from heartfelt agreement with God's commands to careening off the path and reveling in the worship of a statue. It is difficult to imagine a more serious violation of the covenant. Moses, their main leader and revealer of God's intentions, has been absent too long. So the people turn to what they already know. They break God's commandments and make and worship a golden calf.

Apostasy Abounds

We might wonder about such a turn of events, but we need look no further than our own lives. Suppose that we have a significant spiritual experience that draws us close to God where the Holy One is revealed deeply to us. That revelation inspires us and calls us to a commitment. Then we become anxious, scared, or tempted, and we move away from God. The consequences of our moving away from God may take many forms. Putting something else in God's place then becomes our "golden calf."

We know all too well that the consequences of our transgressions linger in our relationships and beg for our attention. A recovering alcoholic may "slip off the wagon" and drive drunk, causing a fatal accident. A life ends and many others are affected. A parent who is trying to deal with anger "loses it" and strikes out emotionally or physically at her child. A relationship is damaged where trust was just beginning to find a home. In either scenario there are long-term consequences for community and family life. Surely people can receive forgiveness from God, yet their actions send out ripples that will require healing for many others. Human failings often have an impact on people across generations. Even though we might not interpret the language of Exodus 34:7 in a literal sense, we acknowledge that human sin lingers among us until we experience healing for our souls. Such healing sometimes takes several generations.

God's Presence
In Exodus 33, God's people continue to deal with the long-term consequences of sin and the divine response to that sin. How will Yahweh relate to these stiff-necked people? Will Yahweh be present with Israel or not? This is a real crisis for God's people, for after summarizing the promise of their relationship, God declares: "I will not go up among you, or I would consume you on the way, for you are a stiff-necked people" (33:3b).

The people mourn. Their grief is real. They wonder what will happen if Yahweh doesn't go with them to the Promised Land. Can they really be the nation of Israel if God is not present among them? Such questions cut to the heart of the people's very identity. Moses persists by talking with God until he receives assurance that God will be present with them as fully as possible.

As part of God's creation, we need to know that God will not abandon us, regardless of the situation. Even after all they have been through with Creator Yahweh, the people seek assurance that God is with them. Perhaps Moses, who was left in a basket on a river as an infant, might recall that he was once abandoned and alone. Moses is aware that this group of former slaves could easily become "no people" again without God to lead them. He pleads until God promises to let Moses see God's glory. God will reveal as much as Moses can stand.

God's Nature
These chapters in Exodus abound with clues about the nature of

God. Brueggeman notes that the amazing response of God to the calf crisis is at the heart of biblical faith. God's language of continued faithfulness is incredible in light of the way Israel turned away from Yahweh. God tells the people to "Go, leave this place . . . go to the land which I swore to Abraham, Isaac, and Jacob" (33:1). The journey and relationship will continue. God could have easily terminated everything, but, instead, God holds the people in relationship, even in the very moments when divine anger boils.

In Exodus 34:6-7, Yahweh's nature is more fully revealed. This speech of self-disclosure overflows with Hebrew words that explain God's fortitude and understanding despite Israel's waywardness.

The Hebrew word translated *merciful* is related to the Hebrew word for womb. Phyllis Trible, author of *God and the Rhetoric of Sexuality,* helps readers understand that this describes the kind of positive inclination a mother has for her child. Womblike mother-love is what being merciful is all about. The term *gracious* refers to completely gratuitous, positive inclination that is offered without cause or warrant. It is unmerited favor. The phrase *slow to anger* literally means long-nosed. Figuratively, Yahweh's heated anger has a chance to cool as it travels through a long nasal passage. The Hebrew word translated *forgiving* means to lift. In this context, the term shows that the burden of having violated the covenant is relieved.

These descriptors of God's forgiving mercy pile up in these lines of poetry, but there are also words that indicate that God does not take away the people's guilt. We must acknowledge that God has the option of passing out pardon as well as pointing a finger. We should maintain a balanced view of God's nature and recognize that God has the freedom to choose what is best for the people. As humans, we are utterly dependent on this God who offers covenant and expects obedience and loyalty. Throughout history, God has chosen to restore covenant repeatedly even when we ignore our end of the bargain over and over again. God is in the business of restoring relationships. And that is good news.

Discussion and Action

1. The Israelites relied heavily on Moses as their leader. In what ways do we become dependent on human leaders instead of finding ways to deepen our relationship with God?

2. How do we feel when learning that Moses was partially responsible for changing God's mind? Should God's mind be changed by the pleadings of an impassioned leader? Do we want an unchanging God? Discuss.

3. What happens when we try to produce something holy? Talk about the difference between objects that point us toward God and objects that become like gods to us.

4. Discuss the dynamics of apostasy in this story. What are some faithful ways to deal with disobedience? How might the church reflect the womblike mother-love of God in these situations?

5. Explore other Old Testament passages with language similar to Exodus 34:6-7. Examples include Numbers 14:18; Nehemiah 9:17, 31; Psalm 103:8-10; Jeremiah 32:18; and Jonah 4:2. What more do these scriptures tell you about God's nature? Discuss the notion that God can give or withhold pardon.

6. Discuss ways in which our nation claims to have special favor with God. Does this idea fit with this lesson? Can any group really claim God's favor, or is it only God's to grant? How does your faith affect your views on immigration policy, treatment of other countries, or the United States' conduct in the world? Does your congregation or denomination sometimes act as if you have special favor with God? Discuss.

7. What must you release in order to deepen your relationship with God? How much does the enticement and pressure of our consumer society influence your everyday life choices? Make plans to be aware of what you purchase or use this coming week. Reflect on what attitudes or feelings build up your faith and what pulls you

away from fullness of life in God. What are your golden calves?

8. In closing, give each person a small piece of paper and a pencil. Write down something that you must let go of in order to deepen your relationship with God (these sentences will not be shared). To symbolize "letting go," fold your paper in half and place it in a bowl in the center of your group during a time of silent prayer. Close with this benediction:

As you travel through the coming week,
May you feel God's presence,
May you experience God's grace,
And may you extend God's love to others.

10

Building for God's Glory
Exodus 35–40

Personal Preparation

1. As you read the scripture and materials for this lesson, notice that much of what was already commanded to Moses is now shared with the people.

2. Exodus 36:3 refers to Israel bringing an offering each morning. As you rise each day, pray for a willing and generous heart. Ask God to help your life become a daily offering of time, talents, and energy for God.

3. Study the word *glory* in this lesson. Use a concordance such as the *NRSV Exhaustive Concordance* to discover other places where the word *glory* occurs in Exodus, Psalms, or Isaiah. How do these other passages help you understand what God's glory is like? When have you experienced God's glory?

4. Reflect upon the past nine sessions. Where have you been touched by God, challenged by questions, or inspired to deeper faith? Thank God for speaking to your spirit.

Suggestions for Sharing and Prayer

1. Begin by praying together David's prayer from Psalm 34:4-7. The New Revised Standard Version uses inclusive language for this passage. If you have a different version of the Bible, change the wording if inclusive language is important to members of your group. Invite

people to share about "seeking the Lord" or being "delivered from their fears" during the past week.

2. Share about times when you felt overwhelming gratitude to God. What response did the gratitude call forth in you? What was your relationship to God like at that time?

3. Encourage participants to share reflections on the whole study. Where were you inspired or stirred by God? When were there times of struggle or questioning? Take time to thank God for all the experiences that led you to a deeper relationship with God and with group members.

4. Use Psalm 51:10-12 as a prayer, asking God for a change of heart and spirit. Pause for a time of silence, allowing people to bring their own needs to God. Conclude with the Lord's Prayer.

Understanding

As we conclude our journey through Exodus, we observe how life has changed for God's people. Israel has been on a physical journey. More significantly, they have been on a spiritual journey. These people, who barely knew their own names and heritage, are in the presence of God and have been embraced as God's chosen people. During this session, we will explore how the Israelite people's lives have changed and consider what these changes suggest about being God's covenant people.

Calling All Gifts

Moses extends the invitation to bring an offering. Those who were once slaves and could only operate at a dictator's command now operate from a desire for covenant. The words *everyone* and *all* are repeated several times throughout Exodus 35. The people respond with exuberant generosity. They practically fall over themselves in their eagerness to contribute. Many gifts are needed for this building project and the people are up to the task. The calling out of gifts begins in chapter 35 and continues in chapter 36. There is just too much giving to be contained in one chapter.

We read in Exodus 36:4-7 that Moses had to ask the Israelites to stop giving; what they had already brought was sufficient for the building project. When was the last time that happened in your congregation?

What has happened to these people who were once ungrateful, complaining travelers? Although the text does not answer that question directly, the whole story serves as the answer. The people of God have seen Moses' face that shines in reflection of God's glory. They have expressed repentance, received extravagant mercy from God, and heard God's specific instructions. Their staggering generosity matches God's staggering mercy. In the process of being restored, they have received new spirits and generous, willing hearts. This is the kind of change the psalmist prays for in Psalm 51:10-12: "Create in me a clean heart, O God, and put a new and right spirit within me. . . . Restore to me the joy of your salvation and sustain in me a willing [generous] spirit."

Attention to God's Directions
The Hebrew people have been a hard sell. Throughout the Exodus narrative, the people have experienced deep doubting and resistance at almost every turn. With such resistance behind them, the people are able to follow God's instructions to the minutest detail (Exod. 39). Incredibly, as we read about the creation of the priestly garments, the phrase "as the Lord had commanded Moses" is repeated seven times (39:1, 5, 7, 21, 26, 29, 31). Exodus 39:42-43 also summarizes and confirms this obedient behavior.

This report provides contrast to the disobedient fashioning of the golden calf. Now the people are listening to the divine instruction passed along by Moses, and they respond wholeheartedly again and again. The one-time making of the calf is counterbalanced by repeated reports of the people's adherence to God's instructions as they make the priestly vestments. These holy items are fashioned by skilled and divinely inspired artisans called upon for holy purposes.

In chapter 39, we see an outpouring of people's creative gifts being donated for God's purposes. Such selflessness brings about a deep sense of consolation and blessing. Life is flowing smoothly! When we align ourselves with God's desires for us individually and corporately, we too experience renewed energy to be used for holy purposes. These times of peaceful consolation come from a sense of glad obedience to God.

God's Glory on the Go

In chapter 40, the tabernacle is completed. The closing verses of Exodus describe God's continued presence as the Israelites' guide (40:34-38). God's glory fills the tabernacle. The Hebrew word for glory is *kavod*, meaning weight, heaviness, or honor. God's glory is a weighty presence; in these closing verses, God's presence is so overwhelming that even Moses cannot enter the tent.

Sometimes our words during worship are attempts to control God or define the experience itself, but we see no evidence of this here. The narrator simply provides us with an account that describes how the Israelites experienced the fullness of God's presence. For an enslaved people who once felt abandoned by God, this is enough. Israel has moved from bondage to Pharaoh to a full bonding with God, who has freed them and now guides them.

We, too, know God in this way. In John 1:14, the writer proclaims that "the Word became flesh and lived among us, and we have seen his glory." A more literal translation would be that the Word became flesh and *tabernacled* among us. God became flesh and through Jesus pitched a tent among us. And when Jesus' earthly life ended, the Holy Spirit came to stay.

God desired to be with the people, moving among them while directing their journey. And God's Spirit is ever present in our lives. Surely, if we are asked, "Is the LORD among us or not?" (Exod. 17:7), we can respond with a resounding yes!

Discussion and Action

1. Discuss whether you can really know the depth of a covenant relationship unless that relationship has been

tested. Can you know what mercy is if you have never received mercy? What does this say about our human relationships or our relationship with God?

2. Discuss the notion that the extravagant offerings of the Israelites are a response to God's extravagant mercy and restoration of the covenant. How might our worship reflect a sense of gratitude and extravagant giving? What needs to change in the life of your congregation for that to happen?

3. Discuss what makes a group of people a congregation. In what ways has your congregation been defined by its experiences?

4. If your church has not had a workshop to help individuals identify their spiritual gifts, consider encouraging your church to sponsor such an event. Contact the appropriate staff members to learn who might lead such a workshop.

5. Name the gifts that each individual group member brings to the faith community. How are these gifts used locally and in the wider church or community? Give thanks for the gifts and talents God has given. Pray for guidance about how those gifts might be used more fully.

6. In what ways is God still a mystery to you? Discuss.

7. Take turns sharing something that God has done for you that you are particularly thankful for. Then share what you would individually like to do for God. Consider ways that you might hold each other accountable in your efforts. Or each person may write their act of response on a small slip of paper and prayerfully place it in an offering plate or bowl in the center of the room.

8. Read Psalm 51:10-12 in unison. This prayer is traditionally sung during the offering in some Lutheran churches. Close by thanking God for what you have learned, and seek God's guidance in the coming weeks.

Suggested Resources

Achtemeier, Paul J., ed. *Harper's Bible Dictionary.* San Francisco: Harper & Row Publishers, 1985.

Brueggemann, Walter. Exodus. *The New Interpreter's Bible, Vol. I.* Nashville: Abingdon Press, 1994.

Buttrick, George, ed. *The Interpreter's Dictionary of the Bible.* Nashville: Abingdon Press, 1962.

Durnbaugh, Donald, ed. *The Brethren Encyclopedia: Volume 1.* Philadelphia, Pa., and Oak Brook, Ill.: The Brethren Encyclopedia, Inc., 1983.

Janzen, Waldemar. *Exodus.* Believers Church Bible Commentary Series. Scottdale, Pa.: Herald Press, 2000.

Metzger, Bruce M., ed. NRSV *Exhaustive Concordance.* Nashville: Thomas Nelson Publishers, 1991.

Roop, Eugene. *Genesis.* Believers Church Bible Commentary Series. Scottdale, Pa.: Herald Press, 1987.

Trible, Phyllis. *God and the Rhetoric of Sexuality.* Philadelphia: Fortress Press, 1978.

Resources for Ken Medema's music: Brier Patch Music, 1-888-536-5365 or www.kenmedema.com

Other Covenant Bible Studies

Each book is $6.95 plus shipping and handling. For a full description of each title, ask for a free catalog of these and other Brethren Press titles. Major credit cards accepted. Prices subject to change.

Brethren Press • 1451 Dundee Avenue • Elgin, Illinois 60120
Phone: 800-441-3712 • Fax: 800-667-8188
e-mail: brethrenpress_gb@brethren.org
www.brethrenpress.com